FIGHTERS

FIGHTERS

Jeremy Flack

This edition published in 1996 by the
Promotional Reprint Company Ltd,
Kiln House,
210 New Kings Road,
London SW6 4NZ for
Booksales in New York, Chapters in Canada and Chris Beckett Ltd in New Zealand

ISBN 1 85648 330 4

Printed and bound in China

COVER: Two Mustangs P-51D G-PS1D and CA-18 G-HAEC, in the markings of 23rd Fighter Group, 14th Air Force, during the making of *The Empire of the Sun.* •

PAGE 2: A gathering of Spitfires over the Arizona desert near Phoenix. In the foreground Mk XII Hurricane, P2970.

CONTENTS

INTRODUCTION

This book illustrates a cross-section of those remaining fighter aircraft which survived World War II and keep flying. When the war finished, huge numbers of all types of combat aircraft suddenly became surplus. As the troops went back to 'civvy street' something had to be done with their redundant weapons. Some were mothballed, some - relatively few - were passed on to poorer countries to boost their defences; however, the majority of the ships, tanks and aircraft left over were scrapped.

This massive surge in the amount of metal available for scrapping sent prices plummeting - so much so that many aircraft were simply pushed off aircraft carriers into the sea as it was cheaper to dispose of them than bring them home where aircraft that cost thousands of pounds to build were being disposed of for a small amount of money.

The majority of the aircraft that went to the scrap man were indeed scrapped; a few were bought by ex-military pilots from a sense of nostalgia, others - especially transport types - were found alternative uses.

It was not until the 1960s and 1970s that a new generation began to look back with interest at the events of World War II. By this time the majority of these artefacts of war had been eliminated. As this wider sense of nostalgia grew, preservation became a heritage issue and the number of people interested increased from just the original crews to include museums and preservation groups

Few countries had an active preservation policy at the end of the war. In fact the Allies actively proceeded to destroy German and Japanese implements of war so that they could not be used again. While these policies can be understood, with hindsight it is a shame that no consideration was given for future generations as many important aircraft types have been lost.

New generations of collectors emerged and began to collect whatever they could find - from pieces still relatively intact in scrapyards through to chunks of wreckage from crashes. Fortunately a number of wealthy businessmen also began to take an interest, either through a genuine feeling for aircraft or as a potential investment. For whatever reason, these people had the resources to recover some of these aircraft and start to restore them.

In the meantime, air forces that had taken delivery of ex-World War II types were starting to re-equip with more modern aircraft thus freeing the older airframes for collectors. As the interest grew, so did the prices, especially for airworthy aircraft, notably those with some combat experience, in particular those with recorded kills. Before long restoration had become an industry with a strong market in components.

While there were many 'cowboys' in the early days, most restorers have earned a good name for the quality of their work. But with fewer suitable hulks the prices have soared. It is possible to spend anything up to £500,000 on getting the remains of an aircraft restored to full airworthiness.

The opening up of Russia and the Iron Curtain countries, however, has brought new life to the market making substantial numbers of hitherto lost types available once more. Hopefully, future editions of this book will include an even wider selection of types. Recent discoveries in Russia have included examples of the Hawker Hurricane, Curtiss P-40 Hawk family, Messerschmitt Bf109 and Bf110, Focke-Wulf Fw189 and Fw190, Junkers Ju87 Stuka and Ju88 and Bell P-39 Airacobra. Most of these have already been recovered. While not all will be restored to flying condition, some have already started down that expensive trail. In addition, the knowledge gained from these aircraft restorations and the availability of new parts is also of benefit to 'static' museums.

Also in Russia, Moscow-based Strela has found it viable to reopen its production line and build 20 brand new Yakovlev Yak-3 fighters. In addition an order for three Japanese Mitsubishi A6M Zeros has been placed. Perhaps this type of operation could be a source of aircraft that have long since been considered extinct.

In the meantime restorers around the world are working on providing a variety of types that were last seen in the air around the end of World War II. These include the Polikarpov I-16 and I-153, Nakajima Ki43 Hayabusa (better known by its reporting name 'Oscar'), Hawker Tempest, Yakovlev Yak-1 and Yak-9, and the Lavochkin La-11.

The pros and cons of restoration to airworthy status versus just preservation are endless. While it is true to say that flying the last example of any aircraft type risks its total destruction in an accident, it is also true that without a collector's resources it is probable that the aircraft would not have reached the public view. Many museums, for example, have semi-complete aircraft or hulks in deep storage. These stand very little chance of seeing the light of day and a number will be deteriorating beyond restoration. On top of this, storage is not completely safe as was found on 15 February 1993 when the Canadian Warplane Heritage lost its Hurricane, Avenger and Stinson Voyager, as well as the CAF Spitfire, in a fire which also destroyed records and archives. The San Diego Aerospace Museum, too, suffered a fire in 1977. Airshows create a large amount of interest and bring in a lot of money to help restoration. Flying aircraft are more likely to be seen by larger numbers of people at an airshow than those static in a museum. It's also true that the safety requirements of an airworthy aircraft inevitably mean that it will be well cared for.

At the end of this book there is a list of airshow organisers, collectors and museums whom you can contact to find out more about seeing aircraft illustrated here.

LOCKHEED P-38 LIGHTNING

The Lockheed P-38 Lightning was designed as a high speed, high altitude fighter. The prototype XP-38 first flew on 27 January 1939: it crashed a fortnight later. Despite this inauspicious start, nearly 10,000 P-38s were built and the type was to see service with the USAAF and RAF as a fighter-bomber, nightfighter and as the most widely used photo-reconnaissance aircraft of the war. The P-38 was also responsibile for the destruction of more Japanese aircraft in the Pacific than any other fighter.

Most P-38s were withdrawn at the end of the war although a few remained in service until 1949.

OPPOSITE TOP AND ABOVE: **P-38L 44-53186 was registered as N505MH and flown by Warbirds of Great Britain (WoGB) from Biggin Hill.**

OPPOSITE BOTTOM: **P-38J 42-67543 of The Fighter Collection (TFC) based at Duxford.**

MODEL/VARIANT: P-38J

WINGSPAN : 52ft (15.85m)

LENGTH: 37ft 10in (11.53m)

HEIGHT: 9ft 10in (3m)

WEIGHT: empty 12,780lb (5,797kg)
max t/o 21,600lb (9,798kg)

POWER PLANT: 2x 1,425hp (1,063kW) Allison V-1710-89/91

CRUISE SPEED: 290mph (467km/h)

MAXIMUM SPEED: 414mph (666km/h) at 25,000ft (7,620m)

CEILING: 44,000ft (13,410m)

NORMAL RANGE: 475 miles (764km)

ARMAMENT: 1x 20mm cannon
4x 0.50in (12.7mm) machine-guns
up to 3,200lb (1,451kg) bombs

TOP AND RIGHT: Built in 1943, 42-67543 was used as a trainer and also flown by Nos 36 and 37 PR Squadrons. It was struck off charge in 1945. Acquired by Duxford-based TFC in 1987 from 'Lefty' Gardner and restored by Fighter Rebuilders at Chino, the aircraft flew again in 1992 as NX3145X. Subsequently shipped to the UK the aircraft is now finished as KI-S *California Cutie* of the 20th Fighter Group, 8th Air Force based at Kingscliffe, Northants in 1944.

ABOVE: Nose art applied to P-38L 44-53186.

OPPOSITE: The unpainted TFC 42-67543/NX3145X flown in 1992.

ABOVE: The fearsome P-40 of the French 'Flying Legends' with its painted shark's teeth.

OPPOSITE: John Paul's Kittyhawk IA is painted in the colours of No 112 Squadron, RAF when based in the Middle East.

CURTISS P-40 WARHAWK/ KITTYHAWK/TOMAHAWK

The Curtiss XP-40 prototype was actually an early production P-36 fitted with a supercharged 1,160hp Allison V-1710-9 engine and first took to the air on 14 October 1938. The P-40 was not a particularly outstanding type but initial orders placed in 1939 were quickly turned into aircraft as the P-36 production line already existed. Its availability meant the Warhawk - as all USAAC/USAAF P-40s became named - was the USAAF standard fighter when the US entered World War II in 1941.

The P-40 earned its fame when Maj-Gen Claire Chennault formed the American Volunteer Group - later better known as the 'Flying Tigers'. This mercenary force, consisting of three P-40 Tomahawk squadrons, operated in China to protect airfields and supply lines prior to the Japanese invasion of Indochina. Outmatched by the Japanese Zero, the P-40 relied on surprise hit-and-run tactics and despite poor support against a vastly superior enemy the 'Flying Tigers' were able to shoot down 286 Japanese aircraft for the loss of only eight of their own.

Early orders for the P-40 came from the USAAC/USAAF and the French air force but France was overrun by the Germans before deliveries commenced. Desperate for aircraft to slow down the German military advance before they reached and crossed the Channel, the RAF took delivery of the French P-40s, which they operated as the Tomahawk. Additional RAF orders followed and these models were called Kittyhawks in RAF service. Later models were able to carry fuel tanks or bombs for the ground-attack role.

MODEL/VARIANT:	P-40N
WINGSPAN :	37ft 4in (11.38m)
LENGTH:	33ft 4in (10.16m)
HEIGHT:	12ft 4in (3.76m)
WEIGHT:	empty 6,200lb (2,812kg)
	max r/o 11,400lb (5,171kg)
POWER PLANT:	1x 1,200hp (895kW) Allison V-1710-81
CRUISE SPEED:	288mph (463km/h)
MAXIMUM SPEED:	343mph (553km/h) at 15,000ft(4,470m)
CEILING:	31,000ft (9,450m)
NORMAL RANGE:	1,080 miles (1,739km)
ARMAMENT:	6x 0.50in (12.7mm) machine-guns
	1,500lb (680kg) bombs

When production was wound down in November 1944, a total of 13,783 P-40s had been built. Besides the USAAF and RAF the aircraft was flown by Australian, Canadian, Chinese, New Zealand, Russian and South African air forces and served in every operational theatre of the war. This is a fine testimony to the pilots who flew what was a rugged and dependable, if not outstanding, aircraft.

ABOVE: Kittyhawk IA in formation with the OFMC Spitfire IX when based at Duxford with the Hannas. AK933 (c/n 15404) was built for the RAF but diverted to the RCAF as No 1057. Initially bought by Canadian Bob Warden when surplus, ownership changed several times until the aircraft was acquired by John Paul, her American owner. Following a rebuild, N94466 was painted in RAF markings and flown for several years in the UK by the OFMC. She has now returned to the USA where she has even participated in the Reno Air Races.

OPPOSITE TOP: The TFC P-40M is now owned by Flying Legends with whom she is registered F-AZPI and painted up as a Flying Tiger.

OPPOSITE BOTTOM: When with the TFC this P-40M was painted in No 112 Squadron markings. Seen here with the cowling removed exposing the Allison V-1710 inline piston engine, 43-5802 (c/n 27490) was one of a batch of 15 P-40Ms supplied to the RCAF (serial RCAF No 840). Purchased as surplus for $50 by American Vance B Roberts with whom she was registered N1233N, the aircraft exchanged hands frequently before being acquired by Tom Camp in 1981. Following a lengthy full restoration to airworthy condition she was purchased by TFC in 1986, shipped to Duxford and given the RAF serial FR870 and a 1943 Western Desert colour scheme.

TOP: During World War II P-47 squadrons were tasked with escort duties, primarily watching over Boeing B-17s on their bombing missions. This photograph revives memories of such missions as TFC's P-47 is about to take-off with B-17 Flying Fortress *Sally B* behind. It also gives a good comparison of the size difference: the P-47 was the largest and heaviest single-seat fighter of the time.

ABOVE: The characteristic P-47 take-off with one undercarriage leg folding before the other.

OPPOSITE: Registered N47DD and based at Duxford, TFC's P-47M is painted to represent the aircraft (226671) of Lt Ban Mayo of 82nd Fighter Squadron, 78th Fighter Group. It is named *No Guts - No Glory*.

REPUBLIC P-47 THUNDERBOLT

The initial Republic P-47 design was for a light fighter and was based on the Seversky P-35 and P-43. The end product - actually based on the entirely new XP-47B prototype - learnt from experience in Europe and was substantially heavier. It was based around the 2,000hp Pratt & Whitney R-2800 Double Wasp which was the most powerful engine then available. The design was accepted and followed a week later with a production order for 773 aircraft. The XP-47B first flew on 6 May 1941 and soon displayed its potential.

The P-47 entered service with the 8th Air Force in November 1942 as a long-range escort fighter and flew its first mission on 8 April 1943 escorting Boeing B-17 Flying Fortresses. Encounters with the Luftwaffe showed that these early P-47Bs lacked both performance and manoeuvrability at low altitude and - most importantly for a long-range escort fighter - they also lacked range. Modifications followed and the resulting P-47C had provision for a centrally-mounted fuel tank thus enabling it to escort bombers deep into Germany.

The largest and heaviest fighter of the war, its powerful turbo-supercharged engine dragged it up to 15,000ft in six minutes. Usually flying high over the bomber formations the P-47 could dive at speeds just over 500mph to pounce on attacking enemy fighters. The P-47 was also used in the ground-attack role when it could be fitted with up to 2,500lb of bombs. Development progressed to the P-47D which was the main production variant. The RAF took delivery of the first of its P-47s - early series D aircraft - in May 1944; they were utilised mainly in Burma for ground-attack.

From March 1943 through to the end of the war in 1945 the P-47 flew some 546,000 sorties on all fronts and destroyed 7,067 enemy aircraft. A total of 15,683 had been built when production ceased in December 1945. They were operated by the USAAF, the RAF (830 in total named the Thunderbolt I and II) and the Free French, Russian, Brazil and Mexican air forces.

MODEL/VARIANT:	P-47N
WINGSPAN :	42ft 7in (12.98m)
LENGTH:	36ft 1in (11m)
HEIGHT:	14ft 7in (4.44m)
WEIGHT:	empty 11,000lb (4,990kg)
	max t/o 20,700lb (9,389kg)
POWER PLANT:	1x 2,800hp (2,088kW) P&W R-2800-77 radial
CRUISE SPEED:	300mph (483km/h)
MAXIMUM SPEED:	467mph (752km/h) at 32,500ft (9,905m)
CEILING:	43,000ft (13,105m)
NORMAL RANGE:	800 miles (1,287km)
ARMAMENT:	6x or 8x 0.50in (12.7mm) machine-guns
	2,000lb (907kg) bombs
	or 10.5in (127mm) rockets

ABOVE: In 1947, P-47N N47TB was one of a number of P-47s that were supplied by the USA to 11 South and Central American countries which had signed the Rio Reciprocal Assistance Treaty. During the early 1950s N47TB saw service with the Puerto Rican Air National Guard during which time it was loaned to the CIA and in turn provided to the Nicaraguan Government along with five other P-47s. Flown to a secret base but not handed over to the Nicaraguan Air Force, these aircraft were to be used by CIA-backed revolutionaries to oust the left wing Guatemalan government of the time.

Piloted by mercenaries hired by the CIA and led by a World War II veteran, Navy pilot Jerry DeLarm, these F-47s (in 1947 the 'P' for Pursuit was changed to 'F' for fighter) attacked Guatemala from Honduras. Researcher and artist Robert St Vincent is certain that N47TB is the very mount of Jerry DeLarm who, on 18 June 1954, strafed and bombed various Guatemalan military installations including the Castileo Matamoros (Defence Ministry). Within three weeks the new CIA-backed president took office. Five of the six F-47s were then delivered to Nicaragua but DeLarm's aircraft remained in Guatemala until it was traded to Nicaragua for an ex-Swedish Mustang.

On 11 January 1955 Nicaraguan President Samoza decided to invade Costa Rica and it is claimed that one of the aircraft taking part in the attacks was a P-47 without markings - Jerry DeLarm's aircraft, probably flown by him in person. The Costa Rican ambassador requested assistance from the US and on 16 January four F-51 Mustangs of the Texas ANG were flown out. The following day the F-51s were in action flown by Costa Rican pilots and were credited with thwarting the inva-

sion. However, it was at a cost - one of the F-51s failed to return. When the wreck was found it was riddled with heavy calibre bullet holes and the pilot was dead. Although there were no witnesses to the dogfight, there is reasonable evidence to suggest that it was DeLarm's F-47 that shot the F-51 down. If this is so, it was the final recorded air-to-air combat involving a Thunderbolt.

In 1962 the Nicaraguan Air Force declared the Thunderbolts surplus and so three Confederate Air Force (CAF) colonels flew down to view them. They were in a poor state with only three relatively intact. The best looking aircraft was selected for possible purchase but there were no volunteers to demonstrate its airworthiness until a figure emerged from the jungle, climbed in, started up, ran the engine and then took-off. After the flight the pilot climbed out and disappeared once more into the jungle. Taken aback the three colonels concluded the deal and the Thunderbolt was flown back to Texas on 7 February 1963. Several years later the colonels were to discover that the pilot was DeLarm and the aircraft one specially maintained for him - perhaps the same one he had flown in those revolutionary days?

In 1970 N47TB suffered major damage and was repaired only after considerable sponsorship by Col Tom Holman. It started flying agin six years later and continued to be displayed until the mid-1980s when operating funds ran short. In 1987 additional sponsors were attracted in the form of Colonels Linda Finch and John Luther and the aircraft was fully restored.

N47TB has now been painted to represent an aircraft of 63rd Fighter Squadron, 56th Fighter Group which was part of the 8th Air Force in Europe.

ABOVE: N47DD is a composite restoration with a P-47N fuselage recovered from Republic workshops and major components from P-47M 45-49192. After a number of attempts at restoration had failed, the various parts were purchased by TFC and completed by Fighter Rebuilders at Chino in 1985.

ABOVE: P-51D G-PSID of WoGB and CA-18 G-HAEC of the OFMC painted for their appearance in *The Empire of the Sun*.

LEFT: P-51D 45-11371 was one of the surplus USAF Mustangs supplied to Nicaragua in 1958 as FAN121. Demobbed in 1963 and registered N1051S, she changed hands a number of times before being acquired by Myric Aviation in 1987. Painted in the wartime markings of Lt-Col Stewart, CO of 336th Fighter Squadron, 4th Fighter Group, 8th Air Force when based at Debden, she was acquired by the US Army Air Corps Museum, Cape May airport, NJ; she was lost during display in 1995.

OPPOSITE: P-51D 44-74008 was one of a batch of ex-USAF Mustangs supplied to Canada. In RCAF service as No 9274 until 1966, the aircraft was sold to M N Bostick of Waco, Texas with a registration of N8676E. After a number of changes of ownership she was acquired by Intrepid Aviation and was registered N51RR. The markings are those of 336th Fighter Squadron.

NORTH AMERICAN
P-51 MUSTANG

The North American P-51 Mustang was originally designed to meet an urgent RAF need for a new fighter to join Hurricanes and Spitfires in the defence of Britain against a German invasion. Just 120 days were given to produce a result and with three days to spare a prototype was built - the NA-73X - which first flew on 26 October 1940.

Named Mustang, RAF deliveries started in November 1941 but the engine lacked the power necessary for a successful high altitude fighter and the aircraft were transferred to the ground-attack and tactical reconnaissance roles.

The USAAF came to the same conclusion and parallel trials were undertaken in the UK and USA to fit Merlin engines into the Mustang airframe. The improvement was staggering and at last the aircraft performed as a high altitude fighter should. During trials, the XP-51B typically reached 20,000ft in 5min 54sec, 3min 6sec faster than the original P-51A.

The P-51B flew its first USAAF mission in December 1943 with the 8th Air Force. As the design improved further so did the orders and nearly 8,000 of the P-51D were built. The P-51 rapidly became recognised as a fearsome adversary by German and Japanese pilots - one of the best Allied aircraft of the war. Its long endurance enabled it to fly over Berlin and Tokyo escorting Allied bombers and its dogfighting performance meant that it packed a punch when it got there. Some 15,000 P-51s were built

MODEL/VARIANT: P-51D

WINGSPAN : 37ft 0.25in (11.28m)

LENGTH: 32ft 3in (9.83m)

HEIGHT: 12ft 2in (3.71m)

WEIGHT: empty 7,125lb (3.232kg)
max t/o 11,600lb (5,262kg)

POWER PLANT: 1x 1,695hp (649kW) Packard Merlin V-1650-7

CRUISE SPEED: 362mph (583km/h)

MAXIMUM SPEED: 437mph (703km/h) at 25,000ft (7,620m)

CEILING: 41,900ft (12,770m)

NORMAL RANGE: 2,080 miles (3,347km)

ARMAMENT: 6x 0.50in (12,7mm) machine-guns
2x 1,000lb (454kg) bombs
or 6x 5in (127mm) rockets

in the United States, and the Commonwealth Aircraft Corporation in Australia set up a P-51 production line in early 1944. 80 P-51Ds were assembled from kits and a further 120 scratch-built as the CA-20, CA-22 and CA-23. Although some were completed, none were flown operationally before VJ-Day.

ABOVE: G-HAEC and 44-63788/G-PSID with markings representing 223rd Fighter Group, 14th Air Force from the Pacific theatre for the Spielberg film *The Empire of the Sun*.

LEFT: OFMC G-HAEC *Ding Hao!* heads a line of Mustangs at Duxford when painted for a part in the film *Memphis Belle*.

OPPOSITE TOP: P-51D 44-72773 was delivered to the USAF in 1951 and flown by 131st Fighter Group and 192nd Fighter Squadron of the Texas ANG. She was one of a number of surplus USAF P-51s supplied to Nicaragua in 1955 under the serialed FAN120. Bought by MACI Sales Finance Corp as surplus in 1963, she was sold to Will Martin as N12066 and subsequently changed hands several times before being bought by Charles Church in 1986. The markings are basic USAF colours although the registration, G-SUSY, was after his wife.

OPPOSITE BOTTOM: Built in 1951 as A68-198 - a Mustang Mk 22 for the RAAF - this aircraft was declared surplus and sold to Fawcett Aviation in 1962. Following numerous changes of ownership and US civilian registrations she was finally acquired by Flying Legends with whom she is registered F-AZIE. The aircraft is seen here named *Short-Fuse Sallee*. She has been given the serial 415622 and the AJ-T codes of Maj Richard Turner, the leading ace of the 9th Air Force, serving with the 356th Fighter Squadron, 354th Fighter Group.

TOP: A colourful line of Mustangs at a Duxford airshow.

ABOVE: A68-182 is a licence-built CA-18 Mustang. Delivered to the RAAF in 1953 and placed in storage until 1958, the aircraft was sold to F C Braund and registered VH-FCB. She changed hands before suffering a serious accident as PI-C-651 in 1973. She remained stored in a damaged state until acquired by the OFMC and was rebuilt by the Hong Kong Aircraft Engineering Co under the supervision of Mel Rose using components from another Mustang. Once complete she was transported by Cathay Pacific 747F to Gatwick before being reassembled and test-flown as G-HAEC. She is currently painted her original markings.

OPPOSITE TOP: This P-51D was one of the many aircraft supplied to Israel immediately after the war through various covert means. She was marked IDF43 when discovered derelict in a kibbutz with all other previous identities removed. Shipped back to Duxford, restored and registered G-BXIL, by Robs Lamplough, she is currently painted as 44-72216 of the 487th Fighter Squadron, 352nd Fighter Group, 8th Air Force - one of the 'Blue Nosed Bastards of Bodney'.

OPPOSITE BOTTOM: Taxying out for a Duxford show.

TOP: P-51D 44-63788/F-AZFI, painted in French markings with the serial 412471, is now flown by the Jean Salis Collection. This aircraft was previously registered G-PSID.

ABOVE: A trio of Mustangs taxy out for a Duxford display.

OPPOSITE: P-51D 44-72773/G-SUSY is now owned by Paul Morgan and based at Norwich.

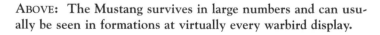

ABOVE: The Mustang survives in large numbers and can usually be seen in formations at virtually every warbird display.

OPPOSITE: P-51D 44-73149 joined the USAAF in February 1945. Assigned to the 8th Air Force in Europe she returned to the USA the following January and, as RCAF 9568, became one of a batch of 32 aircraft supplied to Canada in June 1947.

Sold off in February 1958 and registered N6340T, she changed ownership several times before being acquired from Dr Robert MacFarlane in 1976 by Stephen Grey - the starting point of The Fighter Collection. She is illustrated here painted as 463221 in the markings of the 362nd Fighter Squadron, 357th Fighter Group representing the aircraft flown by Lt 'Moose' Becraft.

TOP: P-63A 42-69097 of TFC taxies out for a display at Duxford.

ABOVE: P-63C 44-4394 of TFC painted in Soviet colours. Sadly this aircraft was lost in a flying accident.

OPPOSITE: P-63C 42-68864 was converted to an RP-63C but little else is known of her early life. Discovered as a playground toy, she was used as a spares source by the CAF for the P-63F restoration. In 1988 she was acquired by Bob Pond and sent to Fighter Rebuilders for full restoration. Taking to the air again in October 1992, she is based and flown from Bob Pond's Planes of Fame Museum near Minneapolis.

BELL P-63 KINGCOBRA

The Bell P-63 Kingcobra was developed from the P-39 Airacobra and incorporated a redesigned laminar flow wing and new tail surfaces together with a more powerful engine.. Two prototypes were ordered and first flew on 26 April 1943.

Initial production deliveries commenced in October 1943 but, like the P-39, the P-63 was found lacking as a fighter, although excellent as a ground-attack aircraft. As such it never found much favour with the USAAF and was only used in the training role.

A total of 3,303 was built with 2,397 delivered to the Russians and 300 to the Free French under the Lend Lease scheme. The Russians utilised the heavy firepower against German armoured vehicles and it is thought that some ex-Russian P-63s were even used by the communists early on in the Korean War. The French continued to use the P-63 after the war and some saw action in Indochina up to 1951.

The main USAAF use for the Kingcobra was in a most unusual role. The RP-63A/63C/63G variants were used as aerial gunnery targets. All armament was removed, all skin produced in duralumin alloy; bulletproof windows were installed, steel grills and guards were fitted over engine intakes and exhaust and the

MODEL/VARIANT:	P-63A
WINGSPAN :	38ft 4in (11.68m)
LENGTH:	32ft 8in (9.96m)
HEIGHT:	12ft 7in (3.84m)
WEIGHT:	empty 6,375lb (2,892kg)
	max t/o 10,500lb (4,763kg)
POWER PLANT:	1x 1,325hp (988kW) Allison V-1710-93
CRUISE SPEED:	378mph (608km/h)
MAXIMUM SPEED:	410mph (660km/h) at 25,000ft (7,620m)
CEILING:	43,000ft (13,103m)
NORMAL RANGE:	450 miles (724km)
ARMAMENT:	1x 37mm M4 cannon
	4x 0.50in (12.7mm) machine-guns
	1,566lb (711kg) bombs

propeller was given thicker walls. They were flown as live targets for other aircraft firing frangible bullets. A total of 332 of these variants was built and the survivors redesignated QF-63s in 1948.

OPPOSITE TOP: Close up of TFC P-63C 44-4394 showing the gun barrel protruding from the spinner and the uniquely positioned carburettor air intake just aft of the canopy.

OPPOSITE BOTTOM: P-63A 42-69097 was built at Buffalo, New York and delivered to the USAAF in May 1944. She was struck off charge in October 1945, acquired by Alfred Whiteside and took part in the Bendix races registered NX52113 and named *Kismet*. Placed in storage in 1952, she changed hands a few times and was eventually bought by TFC. Then followed a full restoration at Duxford prior to her public debut with 'Trussst Me' nose art in 1994.

ABOVE: TFC P-63A 42-69097 lands after a display at Duxford.

TOP, ABOVE AND OPPOSITE: The history of FM-2 Wildcat 86711 is poorly documented. What is known is that she fell into civilian hands as N4845V in the mid-1960s and changed owner several times before being acquired by TFC in 1993. Based at Duxford, she currently sports Fleet Air Arm Martlet markings as well as D-Day invasion stripes.

GRUMMAN F4F WILDCAT/MARTLET

The design that led to the grumman F4F Wildcat emanated from a mid-1930s US Navy fighter requirement. A biplane designated XF4F-1, it was cancelled as its performance improvement was only marginal over the F3F. Fortunately, the USN kept an interest in the F4F and a new monoplane design was submitted. A prototype XF4F-2 was ordered and first flew on 2 September 1937. It was still basically inferior to the Brewster F2A Buffalo and the competition won the initial order but the US Navy still retained interest. It ordered a further prototype fitted with the 1,200hp XR-1830 Twin Wasp and a two-stage supercharger. This change of engine together with some airframe modifications at last produced the performance required. An additional prototype featured several extra modifications to give greater improvements to speed and handling. Initial orders were placed by the US Navy for 285 F4F-3s.

Export orders followed from France and Greece but before deliveries could commence, both countries had capitulated. A reduced French order for 100 F4F-3s powered by the R-1830 resulted in 81 being delivered to the British Fleet Air Arm (FAA) with whom the aircraft was designated the Martlet Mk 1. The 30 Greek F4F-3As with the R-1830 engine were also delivered to the FAA as the Martlet Mk III - a further 100 had been ordered directly for the FAA as the Martlet Mk II. As orders poured in, the F4F-3 became the US Navy's standard fighter. Soon Grumman was reaching capacity and General Motors was given production orders. GM built the FM-1, which was a four-gun

MODEL/ VARIANT: F4F-3
WINGSPAN: 38ft (11.6m)
LENGTH: 28ft 9in (8.76m)
HEIGHT: 11ft 10in (3.61m)
WEIGHT: empty 5,785lb (2,624kg)
max t/o 7,953lb (3,607kg)
POWER PLANT: 1x 1,200hp (895kW) P&W R-1830-76
Twin Wasp radial
MAXIMUM SPEED: 328mph (527km/h) at 21,000ft (6,400m)
CRUISE: 155mph (249km/h)
CEILING: 37,500ft (11,430m)
NORMAL RANGE: 1,150 miles (850km)
ARMAMENT: 6x 0.50in (12.7mm) machine-guns
2x 100lb (45kg) bombs

F4F-4, and the F4F-8 as the FM-2. In January 1944 all of the FAA Martlets were renamed Wildcats and 370 FM-2s were delivered to the FAA to be operated as the Wildcat Mk VI.

Despite the fact that it was the slowest of all subsequent US fighters, the F4F Wildcat remained in service throughout the war. By the end of the war nearly 7,815 had been built. Statistics show that Wildcats destroyed almost seven enemy aircraft for each of its own shot down.

ABOVE: Chocks away on FM-2 Wildcat N909WJ of Warbirds of Great Britain.

RIGHT: TFC Wildcat 86711 during a display at Duxford.

GRUMMAN F4F WILDCAT/MARTLET 39

TOP AND OPPOSITE: 88297 is a Goodyear-built FG-1D Corsair. Accepted by the US Navy in early 1945, she saw combat in the Mariana Islands when aboard USS *Aatu* with CV-102 before being transferred to Naval Reserve and later declared surplus. Sold to a scrap dealer in 1959, she was saved by Frank Tallman in 1960 as N9154Z. During the next few years she changed hands a number of times and was re-registered as N8297. In 1986 she was acquired by TFC and appropriately registered G-FGID. The current markings are those of Lt Ira Kepford who was credited with 16 Japanese kills. The badge is that of VF-17, 'The Skull & Crossbones', of the Pacific theatre in 1944.

ABOVE: F4U-4 122179 was supplied to the Honduran AF as FAH604 in 1956. Bought by Hollywood Wings at the end of her service days, she passed hands a number of times until 1988 when she was acquired by Warbirds of Great Britain from Peter W Thelen. The markings illustrated here represent those of US Navy VC-3 Squadron.

VOUGHT F4U CORSAIR

The Vought F4U Corsair was designed in 1938 with the powerful Pratt & Whitney R-2800 Double Wasp engine. This necessitated a large propeller which needed adequate ground clearance resulting in the characteristic inverted gull wing. The prototype XF4U-1 first took to the air on 29 May 1940 with an engine which only produced 1,850hp, but the potential of the F4U was soon recognised when it exceeded 400mph in level flight.

The war in Europe was providing new information for future fighter characteristics and the desire to incorporate this into the F4U delayed its entry into production. Extra guns required relocation of first the fuel tanks and then the cockpit. In February 1941 the modifications were accepted by the USN and 584 aircraft ordered.

The first production F4U-1 Corsair was handed over to the USN in July 1942 and VMF-124 became the first unit to be equipped that September. Carrier trials highlighted further problems including reduced forward vision and poor control at low speeds. Modifications followed including raising the pilot 7in (0.18m) which cured the vision problem but by that time 688 F4Us had been built. These became land-based while subsequent F4U-1As were delivered to carrier squadrons.

The F4U flew its first operational mission on 13 February 1943 at Guadalcanal with VMF-124 of the USMC. From then on it was to see service in all the major Pacific battles. To increase production, Brewster and Goodyear received orders to build the F4U as the F3A-1 and FG-1 respectively. By June 1943 the first deliveries of 1,912 Corsairs for the British Fleet Air Arm took

MODEL/VARIANT: F4U-4
WINGSPAN : 41ft (12.5m)
LENGTH: 33ft 8in (10.26m)
HEIGHT: 14ft 9in (4.5m)
WEIGHT: empty 9,205lb (4,175kg)
max t/o 14,670lb (6,654kg)
POWER PLANT: 1x 2,450hp (1,827kW) P&W R-2800-18W
Double Wasp radial
CRUISE SPEED: 215mph (346km/h)
MAXIMUM SPEED: 446mph (717km/h) at 26,200ft (7,985m)
CEILING: 41,500ft (12,650m)
NORMAL RANGE: 1,005 miles (1,617km)
ARMAMENT: 6x 0.50in (12.7mm) machine-guns
2,000 (908kg) bombs
or 8x 5in (127mm) rockets

place. The RNZAF also took delivery of 233 Corsairs of various designations.

By the end of the war the Corsair had flown 64,051 sorties and claimed 2,140 Japanese aircraft destroyed in aerial combat for the loss of only 189 of its own. Production of the Corsair continued until 1952 and over 12,000 were built. Postwar a number served with other countries throughout the world through various aid schemes.

ABOVE: 133722 was one of 94 F4U-7s built by Vought for the Aeronavale (French Navy). She was initially with 15th Flotille as 15F.3 then 14th Flotille as 14F.12. The four French Navy Corsair units flew operations in Algeria, Indochina and Suez. 14 Flotille was the last Corsair unit and theirs were retired in 1964. 133722 was retained as an instructional airframe at Toulon before acquisition in 1973 by American Gary Harris. Shipped to California for restoration, 133722 returned to the air in August 1976 and flew for several years until 1982 when purchased by Lindsey Walton and shipped to the UK. Eleven years later, Lindsey sold 133722 to Jack Erickson of Oregon

and the aircraft crossed the 'pond' once more still in her 15th Flotille colours with Suez Campaign stripes.

OPPOSITE: FG-1D, 92044 was delivered to the RNZAF in August 1945. She flew two operational missions in the Los Negro area but was one of only two that survived to return to New Zealand. Partially restored in New Zealand, she was completed by Ed Jurist in the '70s. She was bought by WoGB, then acquired by the OFMC. Registered N55JP, she is now finished as NZ5648.

OPPOSITE TOP: 97359 was built as an F4U-4 and delivered to NAS Santa Ana in January 1946 and placed in storage. She entered operational flying with VA-13 and then VA-134 before joining USS *Tarawa* in 1949 off Japan and Korea. By 1950 she had returned to the USA and was transferred to the USMC with VMF-2. In 1953 she returned to the USN and served with VA-44 until decommissioning in 1956 when she was flown to Seattle NAS for disposal. She was purchased by Bob Bean and moved to Arizona but lay dormant until 1976 when she was made airworthy as N5213V to appear in the TV series *Baa Baa Black Sheep*. Four years later she was bought by Tom Friedkin of Cinema Air, Houston before she was acquired by the OFMC and delivered to its new UK home at Duxford. She is currently painted in RNZAF colours as NZ5628.

OPPOSITE BOTTOM: F4U-7 133722 in Aeronavale colours.

ABOVE: Corsair formation led by Lindsey Walton in his F4U-7 133722 with the OFMC F4U-4 NZ5628 and TFC FG-1D 88297.

ABOVE: Unfolding the wings on F4U-7, 133722. This unfolding is achieved hydraulically and if one wing is slightly lighter than the other for any reason the single hydraulic system will commence moving that wing first.

RIGHT: Ray Hanna of the OFMC flies a low pass at the annual Fighter Meet at North Weald in RNZAF marked F4U-4, 97359.

OPPOSITE TOP: The trio of Corsairs lined up at Duxford awaiting take off for yet another display.

OPPOSITE BOTTOM: The TFC FG-1D Corsair commences take-off.

GRUMMAN F6F HELLCAT

The Grumman F6F Hellcat was based on the F4F Wildcat with improvements to almost every feature - armour, ammunition, power and ground stability. The prototype XF6F-1 flew for the first time on 26 June 1942 and entered service the following January. By August 1943 the F6F Hellcat was locked in combat with the Japanese.

12,275 Hellcats were completed when production ended in November 1945 including 1,182 for the FAA. A number stayed in service for several years after the end of the war.

OPPOSITE AND ABOVE: 80141 was built as a USMC F6F-5K. On retiring she was displayed at the USMC Museum at USMS Quantico, Va until sold in 1972. She changed ownership several times before being acquired by TFC and arriving at Duxford in 1990. British-registered as G-BTCC, 80141 is painted in the markings of US Navy ace pilot Lt Alex Vraciu with VF-6. His kill markings shown (opposite,bottom right) are just some of the 5,000 that were credited to F6F Hellcat pilots.

MODEL/VARIANT:	F6F-5
WINGSPAN :	42ft 10in (13.06m)
LENGTH:	33ft 7in (10.24m)
HEIGHT:	13ft 1in (3.99m)
WEIGHT:	empty 9,238lb (4,190kg)
	max t/o 15,413lb (6,991kg)
POWER PLANT:	1x 2,000hp (1,491kW) P&W R-2800-10W
	Double Wasp radial
CRUISE SPEED:	168mph (270km/h)
MAXIMUM SPEED:	380mph (612km/h) at 23,400ft (7,130m)
CEILING:	37,300ft (11,370m)
NORMAL RANGE:	945 miles (1,521km)
ARMAMENT:	6x 0.50in (12.7mm) machine-guns
	2,000lb (454kg) bombs
	or 6x 5in (127mm) rockets

GRUMMAN F7F TIGERCAT

The design of the Grumman F7F Tigercat was started in 1941 to meet a US Navy specification demanding a high performance carrier-borne fighter with unprecedented firepower. A USMC order for 500 was placed before the XF7F-1 prototype took to the air on 3 November 1943. Deliveries began in April 1944 but the war finished before the Tigercat could be deployed operationally. Only 288 of the original order were completed before the balance was cancelled. Final production resulted in a further 73 day and night fighters.

OPPOSITE TOP AND ABOVE: **F7F-3N Tigercat 80412 served as a USMC night-fighter and trainer until retired in 1959. Then operated as a fire bomber until an accident in July 1966, 80412 was bought by Bob Pond in 1991 and has been fully restored as** *King of the Cats* **for the Planes of Fame collection.**

OPPOSITE BOTTOM: **F7F-3N 80483 spent 21 years as a fire bomber. Rescued and restored, N5178C was acquired in 1988 by Paul Warren Wilson and flown to Duxford from California. In 1993 N5178C was sold to Richard Bertea and returned back to California.**

MODEL/VARIANT: F7F-3
WINGSPAN : 52ft 6in (15.70m)
LENGTH: 45ft 4.5in (13.83m)
HEIGHT: 16ft 7in (5.05m)
WEIGHT: empty 16,270lb (7,380kg)
            max t/o 25,720lb (11,666kg)
POWER PLANT: 2 x 2,100hp (1,566kW)
            P&W R-2800-34W Double Wasp
CRUISE SPEED: 222mph (357km/h)
MAXIMUM SPEED: 435mph (700km/h)
CEILING: 40,700ft (12,405m)
NORMAL RANGE: 1,200 miles (1,931km)
ARMAMENT: 4 x 20mm cannon,
            4 x 0.50in (12.7mm) machine guns,
            1 x torpedo, 1,000lb (454kg) bombs

ABOVE AND OPPOSITE: F8F-2P 121714 was delivered in July 1948 and flew with VC-190 then VC-61 and VU-2. She was struck off in January 1957 having flown 1,100 hours. Initially she became a part of a museum collection and registered N4995V. Changing ownership a couple of times, she was to become the second aircraft of TFC. Initially delivered to Switzerland in 1981, she is now based at Duxford and sports the markings of VF-41 'The Red Rippers' which was one of the first US Navy squadrons to fly the Bearcat.

GRUMMAN F8F BEARCAT

The Grumman F8F Bearcat was the last US Navy piston-engined carrier-based fighter. An order for a pair of XF8F-1 prototypes was placed in November 1943. Although using the same powerful Double Wasp as the F6F and F7F, the design of the airframe was smaller and 20 per cent lighter than the F6F although still able to accommodate the US Navy-specified armament, pilot armour and fuel. The prototype took to the air in August 1944 and showed a 30 per cent improvement in climb rate. Once the US Navy appreciated this significant increase in performance an order was placed for 2,023 aircraft. Within four months of the order the first production aircraft were being delivered. On 21 May 1945 VF-19 accepted its first aircraft. F8F Bearcats were aboard US Navy carriers en route to the war front when VJ-Day was declared and the war came to an end. The large order was cancelled with just 765 F8F-1s built. Postwar, a number of F8F-1/2 variants were built which brought the total up to 1,266.

MODEL/VARIANT: F8F-1B

WINGSPAN : 35ft 10in (10.92m)

LENGTH: 28ft 3in (8.61m)

HEIGHT: 13ft 10in (4.22m)

WEIGHT: empty 7,070lb (3,207kg)
max t/o 12,947lb (5,873kg)

POWER PLANT: 2x 2,100hp (1,566kW) P&W R-2800-34W Double Wasp radial

CRUISE SPEED: 163mph (262km/h)

MAXIMUM SPEED: 421mph (678km/h) at 19,700ft (6,005m)

CEILING: 38,700ft (11,795m)

NORMAL RANGE: 1,105 mile (1,778km)

ARMAMENT: 4x 20mm cannon
2x 1,000lb (454kg) bombs
or 4x 5in (12.7cm) rockets

TOP: F8F-2 122674 was bought on it's retirement in 1963 by Leo J Demers. She changed ownership several times before being acquired by Gary R Levitz in 1969. In 1972, Gary generously donated the F8F to the CAF and over the next 11 years a fine restoration resulted in the return to the air of the F8F Bearcat registered as N7825C. Restorations like this can cost huge sums of money. The CAF use sponsors to solve this problem.

ABOVE: The Warbirds of Great Britain Bearcat appearing at a Cranfield airshow.

OPPOSITE: The main undercarriage door of 122674 has been used to list all the sponsors of this Bearcat.

CREW:
MARC RUSSELL
HOWARD ULM
STEVE BARBER, JR.
DAVE SICA
KELVIN RAUTIOLA
TERRY YAP

SUPPORT CREW:
SANTA MONICA MUSEUM OF FLYING
CLIFF BROWN   DICK RUSSELL
PAT BROWN   AL SMITH
RYAN DVORACK   CECI STRATFORD
SUSAN FINE   HORST WALLASCH
BOB FREBERG   RUDY WALLASCH
CLIFF HERSEY   MERLE SMITH
ROSS KNUDSEN   BILL BENNER
PAUL KOSKELA   JASON KARLIN
CHUCK LEFEVER
WIL LORENZINI
DON MARGOLIN
BILL MAIN
ELLIS MEAKER
RANDY OAKS
RICK POE
MARK POWERS

A/C DONATED BY:
GARY LEVITZ

SPONSORS:

JIM BASSO
BASSO DISTRIBUTING
RUSS DROSENDAHL
DICK HULME
RON LUTHER
DON NICHOLS
TOM NIGHTINGALE
BOB & GEORGIA THOMPSON
ELMER WARD

TOP: LF363 was built at Langley in 1943 and delivered to the RAF the following January. She saw operations first with Polish No 309 Squadron then Nos 63 and 26 Squadrons as well as time at No 22 MU and 41 OTU. In 1956 LF363 joined the embryonic RAF Historic Aircraft Flight which eventually became known as the Battle of Britain Memorial Flight.

ABOVE: LF363 in formation with a Spitfire PR19.

HAWKER HURRICANE

The Hurricane was designed to the same specification as the Supermarine Spitfire. The prototype first flew on 6 November 1935 and became the world's first eight-gun fighter with a capability of 300mph in level flight. Despite a lack of orders Hawker management recognised the likelihood of war and boldly commenced production. As a result when the orders were placed Hawker's was able to supply the necessary aircraft and 497 Hurricanes equipped 18 RAF squadrons when hostilities broke out. When the Battle of Britain started RAF Fighter Command had 32 Hurricane squadrons which claimed 75 per cent of the battle's victories.

The simple form of construction of the Hurricane meant that the aircraft could be built with relatively less skilled workers than, for example, the Spitfire. In addition, it was a lot simpler to repair damage to canvas than a metal skin enabling lightly damaged aircraft to return to the air quickly. The Hurricane was a remarkably strong design and equipped with eight, and later 12, machine guns it was a potent weapon. It later also proved to be an effective ground-attack aircraft.

Out of a total of 14,533 Hurricanes built, 2,592 were sent to Russia to be used on the Eastern Front. Canada assisted in the production by building 1,451.

ABOVE: Built in Canada as a Mk XII, RCAF 5481 was used to train RAF and Commonwealth fighter pilots. Discovered derelict, the aircraft was acquired by Charles Church and lov-

MODEL/VARIANT:	Mk IIC
WINGSPAN :	40ft (12.19m)
LENGTH:	32ft 3in (9.83m)
HEIGHT:	13ft 3in (4,04m)
WEIGHT:	empty 6,577lb (2,983kg)
	max t/o 8,044lb (3,648kg)
POWER PLANT:	1x 1,280hp (954kW) Rolls Royce Merlin XX
CRUISE SPEED:	178mph (286km/h)
MAXIMUM SPEED:	327mph (526km/h) at 18,000ft (5,485m)
CEILING:	35,600ft (10,850m)
NORMAL RANGE:	460 miles (740km)
ARMAMENT:	4x 20mm Hispano Mk I or Mk II cannon
	2x 250lb (113.5kg) or 500lb (227kg) bombs

ingly restored by Paul Mercer and the Aero Engineering team on the Isle of Wight with final completion by Dick Melton. Sadly Charles Church was killed in a flying accident and on completion of her test flying as G-ORGI from Roundwood, she was shipped to the USA for her new owner - David Price. On arrival she was camouflaged and finished in the markings of No 56 Squadron to represent the aircraft flown by ace Geoffrey Page. P2970 now resides at the Santa Monica Museum of Flight, California.

ABOVE: PZ865 was the last Hurricane built. Completed in 1944, she was bought back from the RAF shortly after delivery and was used by Hawker as a communications and test aircraft. Registered G-AMAU, she continued in that role until the 1960s when she was used as a chase aircraft for the P.1127 and Kestrel vertical take-off prototypes. In 1971 she was given an overhaul and presented to the BBMF.

PZ865 is seen here painted in the markings No 261 Squadron applied to Hurricane I, P3731. This was one of the first 12 Hurricanes to be delivered to Malta by the carrier HMS *Argus* during Operation 'Hurry' in September 1940. These markings have been applied to commemorate those who gave their lives providing defence for the island during difficult times.

LEFT: David Price flies leader to a formation of Spitfires in P2970 at the Scotsdale Airshow, Arizona.

OPPOSITE: LF363 leading Spitfire PR.19, PS853. In September 1991, whilst en route to another show, she suffered an engine problem and crash-landed at RAF Wittering. Fortunately the pilot, Sqn Ldr Allan Martin, was not seriously injured but LF363 was considered to have been written off in the ensuing fire. Later inspections proved this to be wrong and Historic Flying was given the job of restoring LF363 to her former glory.

ABOVE AND OPPOSITE: Sea Fury FB11 N232J (c/n 41H/609972) was delivered to the Royal Canadian Navy as TG114. Declared surplus, she was sold to a Canadian in 1962 and registered CF-OYF. The aircraft became N54M and then N232 with Frank C Sanders, and then passed through various hands until 1987 when she was acquired by Robs Lamplough. She retains the smoke generators fitted by Frank Sanders and flies in RCN markings.

HAWKER FURY/SEA FURY

The Fury was a lightweight Tempest for the RAF. When the FAA issued a similar requirement Hawker submitted the Sea Fury and an initial order for 200 of each was placed. The prototype Fury flew first on 1 September 1944, but the RAF cancelled it in January 1945 in favour of the new generation jet-powered aircraft entering service. However, the Royal Navy was not sure about the effect the jets would have on carrier operations and retained its interest in the Sea Fury. Hawker also promoted the Fury for export with initial success coming from orders from Pakistan for 98 and Iraq for 34 plus a further 25 later on. These Iraqi aircraft were to raise much interest on the warbird scene in later years, for when they were declared surplus in the early 1960s they were parked up in the desert. By the late 1970s they had been forgotten until traced by two Americans - Ed Jurist and Davis Tallichet - who negotiated for their purchase. Eventually their patience and diplomacy paid off with 27 airframes being recovered plus a large quantity of spares.

The Hawker Sea Fury first flew in prototype form on 21 February 1945. This was to be the fastest piston-engined aircraft ever to serve with the FAA. Initial deliveries of the FB10 to the FAA did not start until spring 1947. Only 50 were built before they were replaced on the production lines by the FB11. A total of 15 of this variant was built before production ended in 1950. It was to become the principal fighter of the FAA until replaced

MODEL/VARIANT: FB11

WINGSPAN : 38ft 4.75in (11.69m)

LENGTH: 34ft 8in (10.56m)

HEIGHT: 15ft 10.5in (4.84m)

WEIGHT: empty 9,240lb (4,191kg)
max t/o 14,650lb (6,645kg)

POWER PLANT: 1x 2,480hp Bristol Centaurus 18

MAXIMUM SPEED: 460mph (740km/h) at 18,000ft (5,485m)

CEILING: 35,800ft (10,910m)

NORMAL RANGE: 700 miles (1,126km)

ARMAMENT: 4x 20mm Hispano Mk 5 cannon
2x 250lb (226.8kg) bombs
or 1x 1,000lb (453.6kg) bomb
12x 3in (7.62mm) rockets
or 5in (12.7mm) rockets

by the jet-powered Hawker Sea Hawk in 1953, although a few continued in FAA service through the Fleet Requirements Unit until 1962 when the Sea Hawk also took over this role.

ABOVE: Sea Fury FB11 WH587 was delivered to the Royal Australian Navy in 1952 and served until sold in 1964. Shipped to the USA she flew as N260X with a number of different owners until 1977 when she was acquired by Ellsworth Getchell. Painted in original RAN markings as WH587 she flies out of San Jose in California. This is one of the few US-based Sea Furies that still has the original Bristol Centaurus engine fitted.

OPPOSITE TOP: Norman gives a dramatic display with smoke on.

OPPOSITE BOTTOM: Returning in N232J at the end of a Duxford show.

ABOVE AND OPPOSITE: Iraqi Fury 243 was one of the batch of aircraft bought by Jurist and Tallichet. In 1979 she was registered N26SF and then sold to Guido Zuccoli at Darwin in 1982 as VH-HFX. Passing hands a couple of times, she was bought by the OFMC in 1991. Registered G-BTTA, she has been restored to her Iraqi AF markings and displayed at Duxford.

TOP: Adversaries meet again! RAF Spitfire LF Mk XVIe RW382/G-XVIA formates with Luftwaffe Messerschmitt Bf109G-2/ Trop Black Six /G-USTV.

ABOVE: Spitfire Mk IX MH434/G-ASJV of the OFMC formates with a Curtiss P-40E Kittyhawk. Although not in the same class as the Spitfire some 13,000 Kittyhawks were built compared to 20,351 Spitfires.

OPPOSITE: Spitfire LF Mk XVIe RW382/G-XVIA was transformed from a gate guardian to a fully airworthy aircraft in less than three years by Historic Flying. The restoration was originally commissioned by David Tallichet but by its completion the aircraft had been sold to Bernie Jackson. In 1995 it was dismantled and shipped to the USA in time to make its first appearance at an American airshow at the Gathering of Eagles at Scotsdale near Phoenix, Arizona in October.

VICKERS/SUPERMARINE SPITFIRE

The Vickers/Supermarine Spitfire was conceived by Reginald Mitchell who married wonderful aerodynamics and with the best power source available to get the ultimate performance. The Spitfire was the realisation of Reginald Mitchell's dream. The prototype took to the air on 5 March 1936 and it soon became obvious that this was an extremely capable aircraft. Sadly, Mitchell was to die shortly after and did not see his dream enter RAF service. Through continued development, the Spitfire was to remain in the RAF front line to the early 1950s alongside jets.

In the 1930s, the new methods of construction were hard to master and it was not until August 1938 that No 19 Squadron at Duxford received the first operational Spitfire. When war broke out only nine squadrons were equipped and still only 19 when the Battle of Britain commenced.

When production finally ended a total of 20,351 Spitfires had been built in some 40 different variants with engine power developing from the 990hp Merlin fitted to the prototype through to the 2,375hp Griffons of the later marks.

MODEL/VARIANT: Mk XIVc

WINGSPAN : 36ft 10in (11.23m)

LENGTH: 32ft 8in (9.96m)

HEIGHT: 12ft 8in (3.86m)

WEIGHT: empty 6,600lb (1,070kg)
max t/o 10,280lb (4,667kg)

POWER PLANT: 1x Rolls-Royce Griffon 65

CRUISE SPEED: 362mph (582km/h)

MAXIMUM SPEED: 439mph (706km) at 24,500ft (7,467m)

CEILING: 43,000ft (13,105m)

NORMAL RANGE: 850 miles (1,367km)

ARMAMENT: 2x 20mm cannon
2x .5in machine-guns

TOP: MH434/G-ASJV with a Curtiss P-40 Kittyhawk.

ABOVE: Spitfire HF Mk IXE, MJ730/G-BLAS breaks formation and displays the classic elliptical wing shape of the Spitfire.

OPPOSITE: Spitfire PR Mk XIX PM631 of the RAF Battle of Britain Memorial Flight based at RAF Coningsby. Every two years each of the Spitfires and Hurricanes is fully stripped down, checked and repaired as necessary. When this is complete they are repainted to represent a different wartime squadron. Although squadron markings cannot be seen at this angle, plainly visible are the black and white D-Day invasion stripes. These were painted on all of the Allied aircraft during the invasion to assist in recognition.

ABOVE: The CASA HA1112 Buchon is a Spanish-built version of the Bf109 fitted with the Rolls-Royce Merlin engine. Shown here is Buchon G-HUNN when it was flown as part of the Charles Church collection.

OPPOSITE: Messerschmitt Bf109G-2, Werke Nr 10639, G-USTV operated by the Imperial War Museum at Duxford on behalf of the RAF.

MESSERSCHMITT Bf109

The Messerschmitt Bf109 was designed by the young Willy Messerschmitt in 1934. Its construction and development by Bayerische Flugzeugwerke (hence Bf109) was undertaken in secret. The prototype had a setback due to the unavailability of the planned Jumo 210 engine. Ironically, instead it was initially powered by a Rolls-Royce Kestrel. The Bf109 first took to the air in September 1935 and production aircraft entered service in 1937. The Bf109 first saw combat in Spain with Hitler's Condor Legion, flying in support of Franco's Nationalist forces. In November 1937 a prototype fitted with an engine capable of developing 1,650hp for a short period broke the world speed record, achieving 379.07mph (610.34km/h). In mid-1938 Bayerische Flugzeugwerke appointed Willy Messerschmitt Chairman and Managing Director and the company name was changed to Messerschmitt AG.

Developments based on experience in Spain gradually improved the Bf109's performance leading to the Bf109E - Emil - in 1939: this was to be the main adversary for the Hurricane and Spitfire during the Battle of Britain. Although heavier than the Spitfire, the Bf109 featured automatic leading-edge slats and slotted trailing-edge flaps to try to improve the handling performance. What it lost with higher wing loading and reduced manoeuvrability was made up for by the edge it held on speed.

During the early days of World War II the Luftwaffe's Bf109s outclassed virtually every type of aircraft they met during the rapid German advance across Europe. As well as the technical performance of the aircraft itself, this was probably down to the combat experience of the Condor Legion pilots - a lesson that the Americans were to appreciate later in Vietnam. It was not until they met up with the defiant RAF pilots with their heavily armed

MODEL/VARIANT:	Bf109G-6
WINGSPAN :	32ft 6.5in (9.92m)
LENGTH:	29ft 0.5in (8.85m)
HEIGHT:	8ft 2.5in (2.5m)
WEIGHT:	empty 5,893lb (2,673kg)
	max t/o 7,496lb (3,400kg)
POWER PLANT:	1x 1,474hp Daimler-Benz DB605AM
MAXIMUM SPEED:	386mph (621km/h) at 22,640ft (6,900m)
CRUISE SPEED:	328mph (528km/h)
CEILING:	37,890ft (11,550m)
NORMAL RANGE:	350 miles (563km)
ARMAMENT:	1x 30mm Rheinmetal Borsig MK108 cannon
	or 20mm Mauser MK151 cannon
	2x 13mm Rheinmetal Borsig MG131 machine-gun

Spitfires and Hurricanes that the Bf109s met their match during the Battle of Britain.

Development of the Bf109 continued throughout the war with advances in design leapfrogging those of the Spitfire, each struggling to gain the edge over the other. When the Allies finally caused production to cease, the Germans had built over 33,000 Bf109s in various marks of which the Gustav - the Bf109G - was the most feared.

After the war a further few were built by the Czechs as the Avia S-199. Spain continued to operate her CASA-built HA1112s until the last was withdrawn in 1967.

OPPOSITE TOP: The fuselage and wings of HA1112 C4K-107 (c/n 170) are similar to the Bf109, but this view of G-BOML shows the deeper nose needed to house the Rolls-Royce Merlin. She is owned by OFMC and finished as an aircraft from JG3 'Udet'.

OPPOSITE BOTTOM AND ABOVE: The Daimler-Benz powered Bf109 had a more streamlined nose and was faster than the equivalent mark of Spitfire, though less manoeuvrable.

LEFT: The beautifully restored cockpit of Bf109G-2 G-USTV.

OPPOSITE TOP: Hispano HA1112MIL (c/n 235) was purchased from the Spanish Air Force in the early 1980s. The Merlin was later removed and, using fittings from a DB605 located in Italy and components from a Bf109 fuselage found in Czechoslovakia, this conversion has resulted in the HA1112 now being configured as a G-10 variant and registered D-FEHD. It is painted as the Bf109K-4 flown by Luftwaffe ace Major Friedrich-Karl Muller who had 30 victories to his credit and was the commander of 1/NJG11 towards the end of WW2. Black 2 is owned by Hans Dittes and flown by the OFMC from Duxford.

OPPOSITE BOTTOM AND ABOVE: Black 6 (w/nr 10639) was built in September 1942 in Leipzig as a Bf109F-3 but was converted to a Bf109G-2 while still in construction. Accepted by the Luftwaffe on 13 October 1942, it was collected by III/JG77 and flown to Jesi. Damaged, she was delivered to Tobruk, Libya for repairs but before completed the airfield was overrun and captured by RAAF officer Flt Lt Ken McRae. The Bf109 was repaired and given the markings of No 3 Squadron - CV-V. Several flights were made before the aircraft was dismantled in Egypt and shipped to the UK.

Black 6 arrived at Liverpool in late 1943 for No 1426 Enemy Aircraft Flight and with RAF serial RN228 she engaged in trials and demonstrations after which she spent several years in storage. A poorly attempted restoration began but this resulted in numerous parts being removed and lost. She was transferred to RAF Lyneham in September 1972 for the beginning of a meticulous 20- year restoration organised by Flt Lt Russ Snadden and a small team of dedicated volunteer workers.

Surprised by the success of Russ and his team, the MoD eventually gave permission for the completed Black 6 to be test-flown. Allocated the appropriate registration - G-USTV - in March 1991 the fruits of their labours returned to the air. On successful completion of the air tests the MoD agreed that the aircraft could be displayed for three seasons after which it would be grounded and placed in the RAF Museum at Hendon.

Based with the Imperial War Museum at Duxford - the UK Mecca for warbirds - Black 6 enthralled airshow audiences around the UK, even venturing to the Continent. Unserviceable with a broken starter dog and problems with the 1942 self-sealing fuel tank, the displays were brought to a halt in 1993. By the time replacements put the problems right a whole season had been lost. As a result, the MoD gave a year extension for flying the aircraft although it is hoped this ruling will be revised and that Black 6 will be permitted to continue to thrill audiences for a number of years to come.

OPPOSITE AND ABOVE: G-HUNN c/n 235 and ex-Spanish AF C4K-172 was, like G-BOML, one of the taxying aircraft from *The Battle of Britain* film and also ended up in the Victory Air Museum. Restored in the USA as N48157, she unfortunately suffered a ground loop which ripped off the landing gear. She was purchased in the damaged state by Robs Lamplough and the restored G-BJZZ took to the air again in 1982 only to be ground-looped once again. She was sold as a static display piece in Paul Raymond's ill fated Whitehall Theatre of War and bought back by Robs for restoration on behalf of another owner. This progressed on the Isle of Wight with Airframe Assemblies but prior to completion she was bought by Charles Church. With the work finished, registered G-HUNN she took to the air once more in 1987. Following the untimely death of Charles Church, G-HUNN was sold to the Cavanaugh Flight Museum at Mesa, Az. She has since been fitted with a DB601A engine by the Art Williams facility in Germany and painted to represent a Bf109E, Registered N109GU, although she remains in an airworthy condition as do most of the Cavanaugh Collection, due to the high insurance and flying costs she will not fly unless a suitable sponsor is found.

MITSUBISHI A6M ZERO

Best-known of the Japanese aircraft of World War II, the Zero was used as a land or carrier-based fighter, fighter-bomber and, indeed, suicide bomber. It first flew on 1 April 1939 answering a Japanese Navy specification of 1937 calling for a carrier-borne fighter replacement for the Mitsubishi A5M (known to the Allies as 'Claude; the Zero's reporting name was 'Zeke').

Early production under the designation A6M2 Model 11 totalled 64 aircraft, but it was the Model 21 built both by Mitsubishi and Nakajima which was in service in bulk when the war started. 10,611 Zeros were built by the end of hostilities, but very few examples survived the Allies' fierce determination that all Axis weapons of war should be destroyed.

OPPOSITE TOP AND ABOVE: Zero 5356 was built in 1942. Following combat over the Solomon Islands she was abandoned on the island of Ballale near Bougainville until discovered lying in the jungle 35 years later. Recovered and restored with the help of sponsor Dr John Kelly, the restoration was planned to produce as authentic a Zero as possible but a Pratt & Whitney R-1830 replaced the similar but unavailable Sakae engine and a new propeller was needed. The colour scheme of this Zero represents an aircraft of the Japanese carrier *Zuikaku*'s air group.

OPPOSITE BOTTOM: Despite the number of Zeros built - about 10,000 - the Allies' instruction that the Japanese war machine had to be dismantled meant that the Zeros which survived action were all but eliminated. This Zero replica is one of a

number that were modified for 20th Century Fox and the film *Tora Tora Tora*. It was converted from one of a batch of retired RCAF Harvard IVs. Having spent several years in the UK with Anthony Hutton, this replica was sold and departed for Australia.

MODEL/VARIANT: A6M5b

WINGSPAN : 36ft 1in (11m)

LENGTH: 29ft 9in (9.07m)

HEIGHT: 10ft1/8in (3.05m)

WEIGHT: empty 4,175lb (1,895kg)
max t/o 6,047lb (2,745kg)

POWER PLANT: 1x 1,130hp (843kW) Nakajima Sakae 21 NK1C

CRUISE SPEED: 207mph (333km/h)

MAXIMUM SPEED: 351mph (565km/h) at 19,685ft (6,000m)

CEILING: 35,100ft (10,698m)

NORMAL RANGE: 975 miles (1,569km)

ARMAMENT: 2x 20mm cannon
1x 12.7mm machine-gun
1x 7.7mm machine-gun
or 2x 700lb bombs

USEFUL ADDRESSES

If you wish to see the aircraft illustrated in this series of books, the list below details most of the aircraft operators and airshow organisers who may be able to assist.

<u>UK</u>
Air Displays International
Biggin Hill Airport
Biggin Hill
Westerham
TN16 3BN

Tel: 01959 572277
Fax: 01959 575969
Airshow

B-17 Preservation Ltd
PO Box 132
Crawley
W Sussex
RH10 3YB

Tel: 01293 883213
Operator and Airshow

Battle of Britain Memorial Flight
Royal Ait Force
Coningsby
Lincs
LN4 4SY

Tel: 01526 342581/343414
Fax: 01526 343414
Operator and Museum

Blue Max Movie Aircraft Colllection
Wycombe Park Booker
Nr Marlow
Bucks
SL7 3DP

Tel: 01494 529432
Fax: 01494 461236
Airshow, Museum and Operator

Fighter Meet Ltd
2 Field End Road
Pinner
Middx
HA5 2QL

Tel: 0181 866 9993
Fax: 0181 868 0258
Airshow 2nd week May

Imperial War Museum
Duxford Airfield
Duxford
Cambs
CB2 4QR

Tel: 01223835000 x 212
Fax: 01223 834 117
Airshows and Museums

Old Flying Machine Company
Duxford Airfield
Duxford
Cambs
CB2 4QR

Tel: 01223 836705
Fax: 01223 834117
Airshow and Operator

Royal Navy Historic Flight
Royal Naval Air Station
Yeovilton
Somerset
BA22 8HT

Tel: 01935 456279
Fax: 01935 455273
Operation plus airshow organised by Royal Navy

Shuttleworth Collection
Old Warden Airfield
Biggleswade
Beds
SG18 9EP

Tel: 0891 323310
Fax: 01767 627745
Airshows on 2nd week of month (May-Oct), Museum and Operator

The Fighter Collection
Duxford Airfield
Duxford
Cambs
CB2 4QR

Tel: 01223 834973
Fax: 01223 836956
Airshow and Operator

Swordfish Heritage Trust
Royal Naval Air Station
Yeovilton
Somerset
BA22 8HL
Tel: 01935 455382
Operator plus airshow organised by Royal Navy

<u>USA</u>
Cavanaugh Flight Museum
4572 Claire Chennault
Addison Airport
Dallas
Texas 75248
USA

Tel: 00 1 214 931 2214
Fax: 00 1 214 248 0907
Museum

Confederate Air Force HQ
Midland International Airport
PO Box 62000
Midland
Texas 79711-2000
USA

Tel: 00 1 915 563 1000
Fax: 001 915 563 8046
Airshow, Museum and Operator

Experimental Aircraft Association
PO Box 3086
Oshkosh
Winconsin 54903
USA

Tel: 00 1 414 426 4800
Museum and Airshow

Planes of Fame Museum
14771 Pioneer Trail
Eden Prarie
Minnesota 55347
USA

Tel: 00 1 612 941 7820
Fax: 00 1 612 941 0944
Museum and Operator

Santa Monica Museum of Flight
2772 Donald Douglas Loop North
Santa Monica
California 90405
USA

Tel: 00 1 310 392 8822
Fax: 00 1 310 450 6956
Museum and Operator